Gangsta'

ANGEL WITH DIRTY WINGS

UcciKhan

Gangsta' ANGEL WITH DIRTY WINGS

Copyright 2023 by Phillip Sample All Rights Reserved

ISBN: 9798833148235

CreateSpace Independent Publishing Platform, North Charleston, SC

A look into the mind, methods, and motivations of one of Societies most misunderstood persons...

"God knows a man's heart better than we do! While we see the man for his past and use it to judge him in the present, God knows his future. Bro. Sample is a prime example of what we cannot see in a man's heart. I have seen him do the work of the community, for the community, whilst working and engaging in and with the community. May grace and mercy cover Bro. Sample and all servants like him!"

-Rev. Menes Steel
Executive Director *Sow & Grow Inc.*

*

"He is a good friend of mine and a good friend to the community. He has been a major help in keeping young people away from crime. He has strived to be a good father and role model in our community. I have worked with him on numerous occasions in helping to improve the quality of life for our youth, seniors, the homeless, returning citizens and all who are in need."

-Student Minister Troy Muhammad
Mosque #1 Detroit, Michigan.

Table of Contents

"Society got me stamped,
so I'm gone claim it."

-Scarface

"It's His Darkness That Lets Him Do What Heroes Cannot."

-BLACK ADAM

"When the Black Gangsta' gains political and social conscious and makes the ghetto his homeland and treats her with the respect a true homeland deserves..."

-Malcolm X, in reference to Bumpy Johnson; *Godfather of Harlem.*

INTRODUCTION
By: Quincy Smith

"Thanks for accepting my request good brother. I work with a Gang Violence Intervention Initiative in the city. Me and my team work to provide opportunities and resources to gang members with the overall goal to reduce gun violence. I came across a post* you made about the recent indictment of SMB. Would love to sit down with you to see how we can work together and learn more about what your organization is doing. Let me know if you have some time after the holidays. Appreciate the time".

That direct message on Facebook to Phillip Sample was a few years ago. There was a small uptick in gang related shootings on the Eastside of Detroit, and we desperately needed to make more impact and have the credibility to touch more lives. Building a team of credible messengers is not a cookie-cutter approach. Sometimes it takes unconventional methods to bring the *right* people together to create a strong team of violence interrupters. So, I sent Phil a message on Messenger after he made a post about the indictment of the *S*.even *M*.ile *B*.loods and a member thereof. It was a lengthy post, but I read every bit of it. He talked about the impact his sentencing had on him personally and how he wished he had done more to help him get his life in order before he lost it.

Phil agreed to meet with me at our Ceasefire Outreach Office on the east side of Detroit. Quite honestly, I was not sure what to expect. From doing my own homework, making phone calls, and scouring social media, he appeared to be the perfect fit for what we needed. I got to the office early to be sure he knew I was taking this conversation serious. I remember this like it was yesterday. In he walked with his, at the time, 5-year-old son holding his hand firmly. I felt I vetted him to the point where I had a strong idea of what to expect. I expected a tough exterior; a stoic if you will. But he was nothing of the sort. Phil was very articulate. He was direct and straightforward. The more we talked, the more I heard his heart and philosophy of what he felt was the solution. I sensed a very humble and gentle spirit.

There are times when you meet people and immediately there is a kindred connection, and you just know it's bigger than just that moment. The way he catered and attended to his son to make sure he was behaving well spoke volumes to me. I learned a lot about Phillip Sample that day. I knew he had the credibility, reputation, and knowledge for what our team needed. It was almost as if the role of a Gang Violence Outreach Worker, was tailormade for him. In two weeks, Phil Sample would be a lead Outreach Worker focused on the 48205 zip-code, which is widely known as the "Red Zone", Blood territory for the most part. It's where he spent a lot of time as a juvenile, causing much mayhem and destruction as a Gangster Disciple; interesting enough. Here's someone that would be seen as the "Opps" because he represented the *Blue* side, but Phil was considered an OG and he epitomized what we call in this work, a LTO, (person with a License To Operate).

Never in a million years would I think I would be involved in Gang Violence Intervention work. I grew up a son of a Pastor on the Eastside of Detroit. Going to church every Sunday and Wednesday was my life. What I truly appreciated while growing up was that my father just didn't focus on ministry inside the four walls. He did ministry inside the schools and prisons and tried to touch every soul in our community. I remember having services on our church parking lot in the summertime and people who were addicted to drugs, the homeless and those forgotten about, would walk up and be touched by the message being preached. In the summer of 1996, our church hosted a Gang Summit. Invited as the keynote speaker was one of the founding members of the Crips Gang out of LA. The sanctuary was packed with young people, eagerly waiting to hear what this man had to say. I vividly remember my father at the podium, giving a rousing introduction for Greg Davis, who went by the name *Batman*. As he was called to the stage, Batman was nowhere to be found. The Ushers searched the bathrooms, the church office, the bookstore. Ironically, he was found outside on the corner talking to a group of about twenty young people trying to convince them to come in and hear him speak. I guess it didn't take much convincing, because when he walked in, with him was every single one of those young people to whom he was talking. This single event had a profound impact on me and the way I saw ministry. When you're doing God's work, you must cast that net and go where the people are- *wherever* that might be, even the streets.

A series of events in my life, inclusive of the one I just mentioned, lead me to Ceasefire Detroit, as the Outreach Coordinator. At times I would feel as if I were not qualified for this work or have the influence to make an impact; but my heart is set on the fact that God orders our steps, and when you move with purpose and are driven by love for people, the road appears before you- and this is what lead me to Phil Sample.

In almost a decade of doing this work, I have not met a more qualified individual to do the work of Gang Violence Intervention (GVI). I bear witness to the love he has for his community, his love for raising the next generation and saving our youth from the clutches of death and this cycle of imprisonment. Phil's story gives me hope that many who have a similar story can use that warrior spirit within to fight against evil and truly be a part of the change that our communities so desperately need- Angels with Dirty Wings.

-Quincy Smith

...once repaired, i spent my bid repairing others, tis what made me a target to the Ad Min. And believe me when i tell you, we stood up the worse of the worse and when they left from among us, they were better- and the more time we had with them all the more better they became. One lil' guy, when i was in Level 1 and on my way home, was a lil' dude from my Hood named Sonny. When the Hommies told him he had to check in with the Big hommie, he, like i did when i went through the same thing, was like, "What Ever" and endeavored to ignore the call. I had him escorted to the Circle- he was still puffed up and not readily cooperating. I asked him where he was from, he said the Red Zone, i laughed and said you mean what used to be the Blue Zone- he really didn't like that. I advised him to ask his BIG HOMMIES who Young Phil was. He came back with a whole different posture, like "I heard about you my whole life". Come to find out, his big Brother Michael was my lil Mans from the block, who ran with my other lil mans J Greed and Lil Larry. From that moment we became inseparable. You see, we didn't care what you claimed, this is what made us so STRONG! We, Kerm, Yot and many more took care of the lil' hommies and showed them a level of love they had never witnessed. He was of the most talented young Cats i ever heard on the rap tip, especially after sparring with us. He had a Son, i went harder on Cats with Children- yet our time was limited. i would pull up on him in The Zone and poli wit'm, (when we got out) yet he, like i was at one time, was IN TOO DEEP- and though i knew it, i still breathed on him every chance i got. He just got LIFE and some and i wonder if i went HARD ENOUGH! And nall, i ain't excusing his behavior just like i never excused mine, but i know the HEART of the lil' guy and its Sad. I hope he, like many i know, including SELF, who did the crime and the time and made it back out here to attempt to undo what they've done- get a chance at Life again. Young Co, my Guy.

-Phillip "UcciKhan" Sample Facebook Post (2019)

"You know I got the non-profit organization I was pushin', the S.aving M.y B.rothers? I got a lot I done wrote, a lot I wanna' say, you know, people don't know who I am anymore Man."

-Corey *"HardWork Sonny* **n.k.a.** *Corey Qur'an"* **Bailey;** *from* **Federal Prison (2022).**

*

"Some people look at the street corner hustler and judge him/ not puttin' into context why is it that he thuggin'/ what if his role models be about that head bustin'/ daddy gone mamma blowin, it aint she ain't love him/ she was just too busy druggin'/ the corruption had touched him from a lack of love its sort of like it hugged him/ they turn they nose up, he ain't nothin'/ write him off, keep wildin' til the police cuff him/ now we lost another brother to the system- trap!"

-GMAC; *"HUMAN"*

An Affinity to Bad Men

When she and her boyfriend would fight, he'd leave, the Police would come- they'd leave, and he'd come back. It was never them that got him off her or secured *us*, it was *them*. I remember they'd hang out at the Pizza place across the street and when we were hungry, they'd bring us Pizza and Pop. Yea, I knew of their reputation and felt a certain energy when I was around them; however, irrespective of all of that, do you think, I, at 6 years old, thought of them as ugly monsters, villains or bad men, or Angels, whose wings were not so clean?

Not only did I look at them like *Angels*, but from that point throughout my Life, I was attracted to their type, no matter where I went. My cousin attracted to Hustlers and dope dealers, I attracted to Gangstas' and knew that they were different even when I didn't know why or how. They were always clean and very respectful. I've rarely seen a Gangsta' raise his voice, as Gangstas' would activate on you as opposed to argue with you. I seen the ugly side of Gangstas' early and readily noted the ferocity with which they engaged. Aside of that, they were cool and confident and more than all of that, they loved on *me*. It was always, lil Baby, give me five my man, here go a couple of dollars, you good? As a result of this level of attention and father's absence, I was highly influenced by them. The way they moved was respected by everyone. I not only wanted to listen to them and watch them interact, but I wanted to *be* one of them. Even years later when I went to prison, I learned from old Pimps and Mackin' Gangstas', some of whom I had heard about growing up, far before I learned from Religious Scholars. I was watching certain movies and listening to music beyond my years. Hell, I thought Curtis Mayfield made *Little Child Runnin' Wild* for *me*. I dug the depth, and slickness of Marvin Gaye, Isaac Hayes, and Bobby Womack. While yall' callin' ignorant dumb us down music, Gangsta' music; I call that real life, love, struggle, and pain music- *Gangsta'* music.

In conclusion to this thought, what does it say of society to a young boy who seen so-called *Bad Men*, do more good in the hood, than even the Preachers? And though his lens may be skewed or tainted, as a result of *his* point of view, who do you think he would want to be like?

Portrait of a Gangsta'

Killers are too hard hearted and numb to be Gangstas',
but a Gangsta' will kill to defend Life,
a child, an elder-
Justice; Righteousness.

Hustlers are too stingy and materialistic to be Gangtas',
but a Gangsta' is a Hustler
who puts more value on Principals and People,
than coins and trinkets.

Gangstas' don't steal,
but they will *take*- that they may give.

Gangstas' don't lie,
as they don't fear truth
nor the consequence(s) thereof.

A Gangstas' mind is sharp,
his posture plum and square
his attire is tailored and immaculate,
he is well groomed and polite.

A Gangsta' is well-read and articulate,
as he sees ignorance as the ultimate weakness.

Gangstas' are humble and sensitive-
empathetic and authentic.

Sullied by environment and circumstances,
yet pure, nonetheless
and ever devoted to the Growth & Development
of his mind, body, soul,
house, block, and community.

Gangstas' are *Angels with Dirty Wings.*

"Damn It Feels Good To Be A Gangsta'"

One of my favorite rap groups, The Geto Boys, have a song I dug/dig called, *"Damn It Feels Good To Be A Gangsta'"*. It was a rather deep measure that spoke to the idea that being a Gangsta' denoted freedom via independence, profound self-esteem, indifference to the opinion of others, power, community service and more. Funny thing is, I used to quote the lyrics with a passion; not realizing that I was dependent, in more ways than one, I had low self-esteem due to poverty, insecurity and the lack of security, I was overconcerned with what people thought of me as I lacked self-validation. As a result of all these issues and some, I was utter powerless and sought destructive and extreme measures as ways to not only vent and cry for help, but to also assert, justify and make myself relative and visible in a world wherein I felt invisible.

Clear evidence that a Gangsta' is unrefined, still in the developmental stages and not yet "there", is when you see him perpetuating unnecessary violence, social deviance and not having clear direction and purpose. These stages for the most part occur during youth and adolescence; in fact, if at some point, Growth and Development is not realized and these problems solved, the Gangsta' will not make it to see himself functioning on the level of which he is capable. I have seen many of Men who had the supreme capacity to be powerful pillars of strength, security, and guidance in their communities- irrespective of the fact that they were Gangstas' indeed, taken out the game. What happens is one of two things, either they never refine, polish and evolve and thus fall victim to stagnation in stagnant environments; or they refine, polish and evolve, then at some point regress in mentality and thus activity. Reminds me of a part of our Prayer that speaks about wrath being associated with hearing "thine teachings" and going astray there*after*. The message is clear, the Darkside can play for the Light, but the Light can never play for the Darkside.

Anyways, back to the song. One day, after hearing it a bazillion times, I had been free 10 years after serving 15 years, in my 40s and finally, I wasn't on papers, I had a Family, thus foundation, my bills were paid via legitimate means, I had real, not "hookup" insurance, everything in "my" house was mine, I had three cars with no note, lol and I was using *all* my talents to do some good in the hood. Listening to the song from that perspective was as if I were listening to it for the first time. *Damn*, it felt good to be a Gangsta'. I had been to the bottom of the bottom and to the mountain top to see God. I felt strong, relative and vim. I don't ever want to lose that feeling and glow of raw and pure Gangsterism.

"some got killed in the past.

But this Gangsta' here was a smart one,

started living for the Lord and I last."

-Bushwick Bill

Classic Exemplars

Vito Corleone; The Godfather

Here we have, in my opinion, the most perfect example of a Gangsta', in the character of Vito Corleone, of Mario Puzo's *The Godfather*.

Consistent in the creation of a Gangsta', is the fact that Vito came from humble and trying beginnings. When he was young in Sicily, his father was murdered, as was his brother while attending the father's funeral. The local "mobsters" who killed the father, feared retaliation from the Son(s). In this, when the mother took Vito to the head, or Don of the family that killed her husband and son, in an endeavor to save *him*, she was blew down with a shotgun while young Vito watched and barely escaped with his life.

After being smuggled into America, he grew up and took to the streets as a result of limited opportunities. Irrespective of this fact, it must be mentioned that he developed a reputation for taking care of the common folk. He is the author of the idea of, "a favor for a favor". He took care of everyone around him, which would later garner him the infamous yet glorious name, *The Godfather*. It was him who chopped off the

"Black Hand" of Don Fanucci, who was extorting the entire community. I'm sure to Fanucci's people perhaps and maybe even the law, he looked like a murderous villain. Yet to those people, the weak, defenseless, and pure; he was an Angel.

A loving husband and devoted father, with a ruthless streak that reined terror and demanded respect or consequences. He even returned, in the name of what he would call *Honor*, not revenge, to Sicily where he avenged the death of his Family, by slitting the throat of the man who had them killed. He didn't send anyone, for it is *not* Gangsta' to hire a hand to collect a personal dept.

He died old and successful, playing with his grandson while tending to the garden. From his loins, the Corleone Family is of the most renowned names in Mafia stories.

John Henry "Doc" Holiday; A Gangstas' Gangsta'

The odd thing about Doc Holiday, infamous gunslinger, gambler and Gangsta'; is the fact that he was a *real* Doctor. A Dentist in fact; proof that this character can manifest in any sort of person(s).

The contrast and diversity of characteristics is consistent when examining the ways and traits of Gangstas'. Doc was just as gifted with weapons as he was the tools of his trade. He also played the piano, was well-read and spoke fluent Latin, which is "ancestral to the modern *Romance* languages".

Speaking of romance, his love and devotion to Kate, who was also well-read, spoke several languages, yet turned to the life of a sex-worker, is written about extensively, as was his loyalty to Wyatt and the Earp family. Speaking of which, though considered a bad guy, he fought the bad guys with Wyatt and the Earp Family. A Gentleman, the bullies bully and a Gangsta', whose name many Gangstas' have taken as their own to this very day.

Ellsworth "Bumpy" Johnson; A Man with Many Faces

Portrayed masterfully by Lawrence Fishburne in the movie *Hoodlum*, Bumpy Johnson was considered the Robin Hood of Harlem. Of my favorite quotes in the movie, is when the lady of his life, Francine, played by Vanessa Williams said to him:

"you're a perfect gentleman, you're a poet, you're nice to people, you think about things; and then- within the blink of an eye, you can kill or be killed".

To which he asked her:

"Is there nothing in this world that you love enough that you would kill for or die for?"

The scene was set in romantic darkness with the loveliest music to accompany the moment and mood; yet this is one of the greatest *Gangsta'* movies of all time in my opinion. Plus, it is based on the true story of a man, ruthless with a Thompson, yet graceful, charming, sensitive, and poetic with a pencil. A community activist, philanthropist and underworld Legend who had the heart to stand up to the *Mafia*, in the interest of his people and community. An Angel with Dirty Wings.

*

It is not difficult to see the similarities in the examples we have briefly outlined. If we were to look at several more, we would see the same things still. All these Men come from humble beginnings yet became negatively influenced by society in some way or another. Nevertheless, they all had a Love and inclination to protect their people. They were all, considered bad guys, yet they fought the badder guys. So real and principled these individuals that when they made moves of extreme violence, the most non-confrontational of us found ourselves cheering them on; for we by nature know the truth of the biblical excerpt that says there *is-*

"A time to kill,
and a time to heal;
a time to break down,
and a time to build up;"

Ecclesiastes 3:3

Villains and Heroes; One and the Same

Spawn

Of the few "anti"heroes I am going to discuss, Spawn, or Al Simmons is the most relative to the point I'll be endeavoring to make.

Before getting started, I think it necessary to provide a definition of antihero:

"a protagonist or notable figure who is conspicuously lacking in heroic qualities."

And when asked if rather they are bad or good, I found the following articulation profound:

"Anti-heroes are still good people, but their approach to achieving what they want might be different than what society deems "acceptable"."

In simple terms, according to my understanding, antiheros are Angels with Dirty Wings.

Now as to Mr. Simmons, who became the villainous antihero, Spawn. The short version is basically, he was sent to hell, made a deal with the Devil, and reneged. Though damned, stalked by evil and ugly as ever, it is said that he:

"does mean to do good and doesn't really have villainous goals, but that doesn't stop him from murdering, maiming, or mutilating people to do what he wants. Coincidentally, he has a neutral

relationship with humanity, trying to be their protector, but is still bitter and misanthropic."

-hero.fandom.com

Of the most interesting things I read about Spawn, was how he went back to Hell, killed Malebolgia, the embodiment of "evil" and turned *Hell*, into a paradise- imagine that.

My last thought then, is a question for thought invoking purposes. If that was his last deed; then what do we consider him irrespective of the ugly evilness that got him sent to hell in the first place, and the things he did thereafter?

Profoundly sullied, yet pure nonetheless, tis the reason he never took to the idea of being "Hell" Spawn.

All Angels with Dirty Wings have the Power to make a Paradise of the Hell they come from. And they Will!

*

Samaritan

Having no previous awareness of the Character Samaritan, I learned of him via a movie starring Sylvester Stallone. What made the movie good for me, was the fact that I didn't see the twist at the end coming, as I often do. Basically, Samaritan killed his brother, Nemesis, who was the villain, many years ago. He was living as a normal man when a young inquisitive boy found him. The boy having knowledge of the story, figured out the garbageman, Joe, was the superhero Samaritan. Samaritan took a liking to the young boy reluctantly and went to great length to protect him.

Lo and behold, as the story unfolds, it is found that Samaritan didn't kill Nemesis, but Nemesis had killed Samaritan and he who was perceived as the good guy, was actually the *bad* guy, who turned out to be the good guy. This makes the story of Samaritan, or should I say, Nemesis, relative to this thought.

We all have the capacity to be Nemesis, yet we also have the capacity to be redeemed. When looking at most villains, you can see where at some point in their lives, either heartache, trauma or some sort of ill experience pushed them to the Darkside. Look at the devolution of Anakin Skywalker (Darth Vader) for example.

It is often a fine line between the Hero and the Villain, and as we'll see in our next and final example, one can sometimes be both Hero and Villain at the same time, depending on who you ask.

*

Erik Killmonger

Erik Killmonger, my favorite Hero/Villain of them all. Not sure how many people can hate him, as I understood and sympathized with him immediately. Was his methods extreme and his path harsh; absolutely but let's look at the prize for which he was fighting and the motivation behind it.

Far from ignorant, of supreme blood and battling a sense of betrayal by his own people, he knew and believed in the Power of his people, yet could not understand why they weren't using it to the good of *all* their people throughout the diaspora who were suffering. His plan was simple in its complexity. Return to Wakanda, unseat the current King, use his bloodline to secure the throne and proceed to mobilize resources to wherever they were needed. The downside of his plans was the fact that they were driven by pain, hate and revenge; however, this too can easily be understood when you look at what he, *we*, have gone through.

Salute to the Black Panther by all means, but his mind was narrow and his empathy weak. Even his closest advisors endeavored to encourage him to expand his breast. It took the ordeal with Erik, his beloved cousin, for him to see these realities.

Triple salute to the Gold Panther, who if the story was real, was fighting for *me*. An Angel with Dirty and Scarred Wings. I prayed he would come back in Wakanda Forever and he did, in the spirit of *us*, via *her*.

Angels and Demons; One and the Same
Star Wars

When I was younger in school, I learned about the number line. It was basically a long line with zero in the center and as you progressed to the "right", no coincidence, you have what we call positive numbers from 1 to 9 and as you digress to the left, you have negative numbers, denoted by the minus sign next to them, from -1 to -9.

In the Movies and ideology of Star Wars, you have what is called "The" Force. *The*, meaning 1, not 2 or 3 forces, but *1*. Like the number line, there is a positive expression of the Force and there is a negative expression of the Force. Positive they call the Lightside, and negative they call, the Darkside.

The Force is synonymous to the Universe, God, etc.... and speaks to the dual nature thereof. Now, if the Angels were created by this Force, then they too have a dual nature. If they did not, there could never have been a "fall" for Lucifer and his supporters, who were Angels that became the first Demons- *allegedly*.

Now, to take this thought a bit further, if *Man,* is a Creature, created out of this dual natured Force, then like the Angels and everything else in creation, Man too has a dual nature. Let me expound a bit further.

It is said, and my research compels me to believe, that Man is composed of Atoms. When looking at Atoms in and of themselves, we learn that they are composed of a negative component, which gives it its weight, thus making *it* the part of the Atom that would be susceptible to gravity; "fall" of Man; which is called an Electron, and a positive component called a Proton. We've heard this reality articulated as the Yin and the Yang and for *this* to exist, there must be the presence of *that*.

I say all of this to say, that Angels and Demons are one and the same, just as good and evil are of the same Force, just opposites; however, the line is finer than we think. For even Michael, the Chief of the Archangels, not only "questioned" God for creating Man, but is described as a powerful warrior and destroyer, for righteousness though, and who determines what's righteous and unrighteous, for even those lines get blurred.

The greatest point of this assertion that needs to be considered is this, just as Angels and Men, have the capacity to "Fall", they have the capacity to "Rise". Many times, in fact, it's the fall that makes them worthy and capable of rising to answer a "higher" calling.

"I'm going to call you,
our Street Evangelist."

-Catherine Underwood

The Reason for his Anointing

Prior to delving into this thought, dig this:

"3. And Ach, a wealthy man of Behar, made a feast in honor of his guests and he invited everyone to come. 4. And many came; among them thieves, extortioners and courtesans, and Jesus sat with them and taught; but they who followed him were much aggrieved, because He sat with thieves and courtesans. 5. And they upbraided Him; they said: "Rabboni, Master of the wise, this day will be an evil day for you. 6. The news will spread that you consort with courtesans and men will shun you as they shun an asp." 7. And Jesus answered them and said; "A master never screens himself for the sake of reputation or of fame. 8. These are but worthless baubles of the day; they arise and sink, like empty bottles on a stream; they are illusions and will pass away. 9. They are the indices to what the thoughtless think; they are noise that people make; and shallow men judge merit by the noise. 10. Allah and all master men judge men by what they are and not what they seem to be; not by their reputation and their fame. 11. These courtesans and thieves are children of my Father Allah; their souls are just as precious in His sight as yours; or of the Brahmic priests. 12. And they are working out the same life sums that you have solved, you men who look at them with scorn. 13. And some of them have solved much harder than you have solved, you men who look at them with scorn. 14. Yes, they are sinners, and confess their guilt while you are guilty, but are shrewd enough to have a polished coat to cover up your guilt."

The Holy Koran

Though there are a many of jewels we can take from this measure, I want to direct our thoughts to the point most relative to the question; "what is the reason for *his* anointing?" His, in this context represents, the thief, the courtesan, the Gangsta'! What divine assignment can these deviants possibly serve?

Imagine if God, Jesus, the Prophets, whatever; understood that to reach a deviant people, they'd have to use the ministry of deviant persons? A testimony, come on now, is not a thing of hearsay, but a thing of being a witness bearer. And not only a witness bearer, but clear evidence that the possibility of overcoming issues, adversities and even *demons*, is possible and real. All Praise is Due. The fact that I've been there provides me an understanding that nothing else can; this allows me to be relative, empathetic, and affective. And so, the book calls us to be mindful regarding, "the lease of these". But it's something in us that makes us arrogant and blind to the point where we miss this; however, it is further said that "the stone that the builders rejected; would become the cornerstone"! This is why the Gangsta' has a divine anointing; he has the experience, the empathy, the heart, and the *responsibility* to be a pillar of excellence, defense, and compassion in his community.

I hear you, but what if the Gangsta's don't recognize that higher calling and are darkened by experience and trauma? Great question, to which the answer is even greater, the worst of us, will be the best of us. How do I know? I am clear evidence. If there is Life in the vessel, God is in the vessel; however, to make it manifest, you must be in the proper time, the right environment, be a qualified practitioner and have the proper technique. Don't tell me my babies can't be reached because *you* can't reach them.

They have a divine assignment for which they have been preparing. They are truly baby Angels with Dirty Wings; and I will endeavor to make this point clear.

"I pray the pressure comes back. Sooner or later there will be a savage "gang" of young-ones that make selling drugs, taking innocent lives, and harming our own community a street-sin. In other words, I hope the shit that we thought was cool becomes an offense."

-J.A. Cotton; Founder & CEO
@Big Homies Inc. (Non-Prof. Org.)

From Demon Time to An Army of God

It is an expression amongst our youth today that they refer to as being on "Demon Time". It reminds me of when I was young and in the streets heavy, how we shot out the streetlights in our neighborhood and called it the *Darkside,* of which we were the *Demons* therefrom.

The irony of this line of thought, is the fact that it is driven by the purest form of human nature, which when unrefined and unevolved, looks a lot like animal nature. Being on Demon Time stems from a feeling of hopelessness and thus carelessness. It is a something must happen before something happens type of attitude and energy. I am hungry, mentally unstable, unfulfilled, and suicidal. Any actions, though we can't totally excuse them, that stem from this state of mind must be examined and understood. Nothing is beyond doing when a person is in this space. The sad part about it, is that some of the actions committed in this space have such lasting consequences, that we still suffer them even when we've snapped out of it. The worst thing is an incarcerated Angel, locked forever away from a world that it could be serving because of a reaction to pain, fear, poverty, and unaddressed trauma in its most vulnerable and unevolved state.

How it is possible for a baby, born pure and beautiful to grow to be a menace to society, on Demon Time, must be examined. And if we can garner some insight into that *how,* we may see how there is the capacity for redemption.

All sacred texts, from the Bible, Qur'an, etc., speak of the dual nature of Man. Philosophers have philosophized about it since the beginning of time. It is portrayed in cartoons and is the stuff that makes the stories of villains and heroes so intriguing, for they are really expressions of the age-old battle of good and evil- in *Man*. In this, we are again moved to not only think about the duality of man, but its source as well.

I found, as I articulated earlier, that the smallest elements or parts of everything, including Man, is Atoms. After studying the construct and function of Atoms, I learned that they are composed of both a positive part (proton) and a negative part (electron), as well as a neutral part (neutron). So then, in the very essence of Mans physical make up is a negative element or particle.

Further looking into the physical evolution of Man, I found that the brain stem, or "reptilian brain" is of the first things to manifest. It is said that this portion of the brain is responsible for, amongst other things, "control of our innate and automatic *self-preserving behavior* patterns, which ensure our *survival* and that of our species." I think I stated earlier how unevolved Man and animals are relative in instinctive qualities and nature. Nevertheless, as the brain or anatomy continues to form, the portions of the brain that make way for reason and empathy come into play. We must also remember that it is a process that completes when we are in our 20's. This is why it was ruled to be unconstitutional to sentence a child as an adult, for he is not physiologically thus.

In these expressions we see the presence and capacity to what we call negative and socially deviant behavior. And it is my opinion that a Man is most civilized when civilization allows him to be. Let me expound. Sometime ago it was a blackout in

Detroit that lasted several days. It was a mess and compelled me to think about what if something happened, that lasted for months, that robbed us of our day-to-day resources and things we *think* are necessities? Void of technology our instincts would kick back in. After the immediate resources are exhausted, we would revert to looting and even endeavoring to hunt perhaps- yea, the most refined of us. Unshaven and sullied, we'd began to look like something primitive. The longer the deprivation, the more we'd be compelled to *survive*, at any cost. Would it look like the Purge, Mad Max, or a bit of both? Or would government or a higher moral code in us compel us to decency and humanity? Either way, we have the capacity to bounce back, yet to what degree and how fast would depend on the resources and assistance available.

Now imagine a place or space where deprivation and the lack of basic necessities has lasted for generations. As to the definition of *Ghetto,* it articulates:

noun 1. A poor urban area occupied primarily by a minority group or groups.

adjective resembling or characteristic of a ghetto or its inhabitants (especially in relation to African American culture).

verb put in or restrict to an isolated or segregated area or group.

Wikipedia states:

"A ghetto, is a part of a city in which members of a minority group live, especially as a result of political, social, legal, environmental or economic pressure."

In essence, this is not a place where people are known to thrive. It further handicaps the idea of civilization as the people therein become products of such environments. Resources are scarce and hope is at an all-time low, thus savage behavior, "Demon Time" is the norm. The capacity to bounce back is absent, as resources and assistance is absent. This has been the reality for not days, or weeks; or even months or years, but decades. The Devil has an *in,* to Man when he is hungry, unrefined, under expressed, ill-represented, afraid, without righteous resource or recourse and hopeless. This is why anyone who can't understand the utter necessity for service provision is out of touch and not fit for this facet of social endeavor. It is hard to talk reason or rationale to a population that is starving not only physically, but mentally, socially, and spiritually. These voids must be filled, or violence will continue to be the reality.

To cope with the social ills of environment, we put ourselves further into deviance via coping mechanisms, such as drugs and alcohol. These further push us away from constructive and rational decision making. And then we are exploited in this regard with a barrage of liquor stores and easy access to poison and weapons. Why do you think so many go to prison and find the light of self and return to society with a different attitude and thus mission? That space offers the clarity for pure thoughts, unintoxicated prayers and reflection and thus the opportunity to think in accordance with our nature- which is righteous and pure. The struggle to eat and find shelter is solved, though not in the most ideal of ways, but nevertheless. This I believe is the mysterious way of the Force or God. In this darkness, the Demon recognizes that he is actually an Angel who has been oppressed, de-pressed and suppressed. By this awareness, the consciousness is quickened, and the lights come on. Look and think of the evolution of Malcolm X when he was incarcerated.

From Demon Time to an Army of God? When the lights come on in all those who are considered deviant or whatever, and they realize they have a higher calling that the Life has prepared them for, they'll began to be fueled by a different spirit or level of vibration- Angel Time. Dig this.
The Bible speaks about a valley of dry bones in the book of Ezekiel and how once quickened with the spirit of God and LIFE, though seemingly dead, scattered, and aimless, came together and rose up into "an exceedingly great army", the Army of *God*.

This Army, All Praise is Due, will be composed of the best of us- who came from the worst of us and until this is so, we will continue to suffer from dysfunction, violence, exploitation, insecurity and aimlessness, for if the Sun is out of orbit, the Universe will be in chaos. The Moon, our Women, bless their hearts, will continue to strain their light in the endeavor to compensate for our ineptitude, bless their hearts, but it's *not* the natural way. They need *us*, to Man up, stand up, pull our pants up and put our hands up in defense of them, our babies (future) and communities.

In conclusion to this thought, young Warriors, we aim not to turn off the fighter in you, we aim to properly direct it. Your people, children, women, neighborhoods; need your strength, protection and guidance. Legacy is not spawn from menace, but benevolence. Tookie Williams became more famous for the redemptive work he put in than he did for destroying his community. Do you think the Bloods and Crips would be more impactful if they keep killing one the other until no one is left, or if they unified and took the idea of organization to a social and political level? Will Hoover be remembered for Pitchforks or Growth and Development? Will I be loved for burning down the hood, or building it up? Will your mothers and families be prouder of you in prison or college?

You don't want to be hated, to the contrary, by nature we desire to be loved, accepted and understood; yet we've been traumatized to the point we fear even these most natural sentiments, yet let it be known, you, we, have the power to overcome all of that and when we do, we must articulate and exemplify this to the next generation, this is the responsibility of the O.G.s, this is why you survived. It is thought that the youth do not respect the elders, this is not what my experience has shown me. It has however shown me that they must be given something to respect; and ain't nothin' more, respect or story worthy than one who came from mud and the most trying of experiences yet overcame to be a pillar for righteousness. This is how we purify our wings and carve our space in Heaven. Period!

"Phillip Sample, you are a Soldier for God."

-Terrance Carey

*

"My Father who was a Pastor in the city of Chicago, and my Mother did a lot of work with Gang Members there. Actually, they took a Church that was started there and took it from 8 members to over 400 members and the majority of those members were actually involved in Gangs."

-Bishop Daryl Harris; *Total Life Christian Ministries*

"True O.G.s are O.pportunity G.ivers"

-George Galvis; Executive Director
@ Communities Untied
for Restorative Youth Justice.

True O.G.s

I once saw on Facebook, a post detailing what someone thought was or should be the criteria by which one can call him or herself, an O.G. I liked it so much that I screen shot it and kept it, which was a good thing that I may share it with you:

"1. 35+ years membership. 2. Outstanding Member. 3. Once held a leadership position. 4. Respected by all (rivals as well). 5. Retired Honorably. 6. Advocate for younger members to change their lives verbally or by example."

Be this the standard, I would meet and exceed all of these, save number 5, as I am not retired, nor do I see it in the forecast. At any rate, I love these points nonetheless, especially number 6, as it would lead into what I believe should be number 7. As quoted previously, I heard my Comrade in Oakland talk about how a true O.G. is an *O.pportunity G.iver.* I thought this rather profound, and it made me think about what it really meant.

Opportunity, or the lack thereof is one of the main reasons our babies become deviant. In this, if I have survived The Life and have carved a way for myself, the greatest thing I can do for our youth is show them that a normal life without violence, revenge, prison, fear and hatred is possible; for by way of *this* example, you give them the Opportunity to *Live*!

Further on this thought, I know a many of Men and Women who live their redemption via killing the beasts that created them. What do I mean? I was an inner-city youth who fell victim to Gang Violence and the destruction of my community. After serving a large part of my Life in prison, divine favor would be for me to be able to make a living in the field of youth and Gang/Community Violence intervention. A large part of my decision making was based on the fact that I was poor and void of resource, in this, a large part of what I do is relative to providing resources to at risk youth and youth before they become at risk. A woman who was molested as a child, can sulk and permit that horrible time and space to forever cripple her, or she can raise awareness around the sexual exploitation of children. Via the latter, she would be fighting the very thing that offended her. This is the empowering choice, for this is probably the work she was called to do. All Praise is Due.

To add to the ways and characteristics of True O.G.s, mostly every one I ever knew hated unnecessary violence, for not only was it bad for business, but it was bad for Community. True O.G.s get the assignment, that if home, or the "Hood" ain't safe, then nowhere is.

A True O.G.s true enemies are the things that he, at some point came to realize were the damning factors in his own life; poverty, racism, domestic and community violence, ill-education, etc. If a True O.G. claims any affiliation to anything, it would be principals that speak to these issues and his alliances will be any and everyone fighting these same demons, irrespective of what hood they from, what color they wear, the pass, etc., for victory is the most important thing, for the contrary is death for everybody.

So yea, I consider myself a triple, double O.G., by those standards and these. And I salute the True O.G.s wherever you are, no matter what you claim, for like we used to say on the yard in our drills:

"What's the Key?!"
"Unity!!!"

"The role and duty of an O.G.
is to guide and provide
knowledge, wisdom and understanding
to the lil' hommies'."

-Lawrence "Eastside L.A." Sample

Gangsterism vs. Gang Bangin'

Gangbangin' is the apex expression of self and kind hatred. To reach a point where a color, or the way we fix our hands or whatever, become the things for which we kill one the other is the height of suicidal/genocidal behavior. Gangbangin', next to drugs, is the greatest cause for community trauma; for some Gang feuds have lasted for *generations*. True Gangstas' abhor the idea of Gangbangin', especially once they evolve. Many frown on that part of their past, as they realize that they were instruments in the demise of their own people and neighborhoods.

Education cannot happen amid Gang Bangin', thus a many of Gangbangers are or were intelligent, yet *under*developed.

Family can't happen amid Gangbangin' for everyone is in danger in an environment plagued with violence. Community cannot happen amid Gangbangin', for every event is in jeopardy. Freedom cannot be realized, for though we've already been crippled by a lack thereof, we further encage ourselves when we can't leave our neighborhoods without fear or feeling the need to be prepared to defend ourselves.

Gangbangin' undermines the idea of Unity, which again is the Key to our empowerment; financially, politically, socially, etc.

Gangbangers do not die legends, save for on their own block, amongst their own circle. Gangstas' become legendary even while living.

Gangbangin' in and of itself, has no monetary gain or form of production. Beef interferes with business and being segregated shortens one's range, when the broader your network, the broader your net worth. BMF understood this to the supreme extent- and imagine if that ideology would have morphed into politics, corporations, security. Black Mafia indeed.

Bos up and stop the cycle of self-destruction. Take a page out the real Brothers of the Struggle book. They were from all relative sets, who *United in Peace* for Freedom, Justice, and Equality. Real Gangsta' shit!

"Guns, we don't like to usem'
Unless- our enemies choosem'
We prefer to fight you all like a man
and beat you down,
with our hands and body slam you at-"

-The Wild Wild West; *Kool Moe Dee*

Gangstas' and Guns

A Gangsta' is both Scholar and Warrior and as one can't be a scholar without real life experience, one can't be a warrior without the proper foundation. To ever be considered battle hard and real respect worthy, is to get it the fist-to-cuff way. As a result of this reality, most primitive weapons; knives, bats, chains, etc., were extensions of the hands. To deliver a blow, one had and must get up close and personal. Bones were made and some broken, but respect was earned, even when one took an L, for when we took them (and everybody has taken them) we took them with class, head high and swinging. The worst coward in the world, was one who lost a fist fight and came back with a gun.

Speaking of Guns, they changed the Game and rules of engagement. I personally hate that they were ever made, as I believe in the ways of Sword and Shield; however, I have profound commonsense and the last thing anyone would ever want to do, is take a knife to a gun fight.

The most terrible thing about guns in my opinion and unfortunate experience, is the fact that they are too powerful, unpredictable, and uncontrollable. Most of the weapons with which our streets are infested, were created for warzones;

jungles and the like, not residential living quarters. They go through walls, ricochet, miss their targets and keep traveling.

To be frank, I think someone not only took interest in us killing ourselves and thus wanted to make it easier, but they studied and catered to our psychological frailties at the same time. For how many a weak men found strength in the firearm?

Weapons for sport and or hunting, and even self-defense is one thing, but when weapons are easily obtained, especially by untrained youth and glorified in everything with which we engage, it's another and its ugly. I will say though and I hate to admit it, but because firearms invoke fear and are perceived as tools of power, I have seen firearms play the role of de-escalation tools. Most robbers and carjackers are looking for what they perceive to be "easy licks", the presence of a properly carried firearm will make a predator think twice. In this and as the world is the way it is, I think women ought be armed when alone. I think men, especially those with wives and children, ought be able to address any threat to their persons and/or families. However, they must cease being the go to for conflict resolution and should at no time be accessible to children. Sad thing is, I don't see this happening any time soon. In this, we must be active in raising the awareness about gun safety, teach conflict resolutions skills and anger management in relative and meaningful ways. Gangstas' don't like guns, but since they are here, they understand their necessity, especially when many of our people who carry them consider themselves to be on "Demon Time". The Bible even admonished us to turn our garden tools into spears, which speaks to the arming of ourselves by any means- against evil.

Sad is the Angel, capable of defending his family and community, yet barred by laws and a society that punishes one forever. It was said that it is unconstitutional to infringe on certain rights for convicted felons; employment, fair housing and the right to civic engagement, but not the right to bear arms, of which is of the most fundamental of rights?

A juvenile catches a gun case at 17, does his time, returns to society a productive member of the community, yet understanding the dangers of the community, carries and gets caught with a gun- at 50 years of age. First of all, at some point, something should be in place that will aid him in having *all* of his rights restored and until that can happen, at the very least his past shouldn't be used to weigh him at the present. The capacity to defend and secure is a part of what makes a man a man, thus, to forever take that away, is cruel and unusual. And I hear you, the Law is the Law, O.K., but slavery was once the Law, and it was *wrong*.

Gangstas' get the assignment, pride themselves on protecting the community and have been trained the hard way and are fearless. You would want an armed Gangsta' present in the course of a school shooting, amid other heinous crimes in our communities. Stop disarming the Army of God based on what was done prior to enlightenment.

It doesn't seem, unfortunately, like guns are going anywhere soon, in this we must permit an even battlefield, for I will serve and protect, for it is the reason God gave me the strength and acumen to do so- dirty wings and all. To hinder my capacity to wrap my wings around my neighborhood in the most loving, affectionate, and protective ways, is to impede upon the Will of *God*!

Acknowledgements

Firm Salutations and much respect and gratitude to everyone who aided in the manifestation of this thought. My Wife, my O.G.s for showing me the ways, those whose wisdom I quoted and Quincy Smith for the profound words. Bro. Nez for the technical support and every person and place that'll aid in its mobilization.

Ceasefire Detroit for allowing me a space to do some *meaningful* work in the community. Who'd think all the not so good experiences would be the very things that made me qualified- proof that all things can ultimately serve a higher and righteous purpose, even the dirt on ones Wings. Though I wrestled with portions of the model, the work we did, and you do, is divine, nonetheless.

I must turn the light of gratitude toward every dark and vulnerable space I've ever been in, every bully that chose me and every situation where I witnessed the so-called strong mis or ab use the weak; for it is these things that instilled in me, a desire to fight for the good side and those who can't fight for themselves. My methods are extreme yet come from my understanding of how extreme evil can be, thus my motives are pure.

Salute to all the real grassroots, boots on the ground, in the mud Org.s endeavoring to do some good in the hoods; Detroit Friends and Family, Detroit 300, Force Detroit, The People's Action Network, WE Detroit, Growth & Development, the F.O.I., the Moors, the Solah's, Detroit DAWGS,

Team Pursuit, RAHAM Inc., Caught Up, Eyes Wide Open, New Era Detroit, etc. Though the world may not see it now, but you are all real life superheroes, keep pushing in righteousness and solidarity. *We Are One* as is the Force by which we are compelled and once we really realize that, anything not vibrating in synch with our motion, will cease to exist in our homes and communities.

And lastly, I salute every Angel with Dirty Wings, especially the ones who at some point fell to the Darkside- yet rose above it and now fight for Freedom, Justice, and Equality, rather free or caged. You- *we,* are the most valuable warriors on the board, as we are tried, true and battle hard- yet motivated and compelled by a higher calling, redemption, and moral fortitude.

UcciKhan
Straight, bona fide, unadulterated, Gangsta'

www.uccikhan.com

Available Books by UcciKhan

The Passion of The Life part 1. The Life

To My Unborn Seed
(thoughts, fears, feelings & hopes)

*

Coming Soon

After Birth
(gems for a baby girl befitting a woman)

The Passion of The Life part 2. Death

Divine Insanity
(prayers, poems & letters; written in confinement)

Listen to
Angel With Dirty Wings
by *UcciKhan*

Merch., Music & More

www.uccikhan.com

UcciKhan
(All Terrain)
High-top Boots

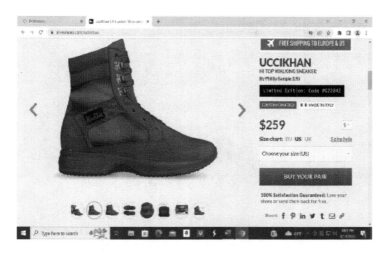

Proceeds go to
www.rahamdetroit.org

in support of those with their
"Boots On the Ground"
in our communities for positive progress

" S.tompD.ownH.ard "
EVERYTHING

Coming Soon

79594990R00037